# The *Beauty* of COVENANT

Covenant Teaching Ministry
PO. Box 83
Malvern, PA 19355
Email: CovenantTM@gmail.com
Website: www.CovenantTM.com

May 2016
Printed in the United States of America

Family and Relationships - Marriage
Religion - Christian Life - Love and Marriage

ISBN: 9780692676530

# The *Beauty* of COVENANT

Mary Walmsley

Malvern, PA

To

my children,

grandchildren,

great grandchildren,

and future generations.

# ACKNOWLEDGEMENTS

I am grateful to Jesus Christ for being my Lord. Through Him
I have been blessed with the love, encouragement and help of
family and friends, without whom this work would never have
been accomplished.

The Covenant Teaching Ministry team: Hartley Connett,
Stephen Schmid, Herbert Wagner, John Heidengren, Morgan
Smith, Jeff and Dianne Moretzsohn,

Julia Belknap, Diane Gibson and Janet Robinson, companions
in prayer,

Holly Puett, whose simple suggestion opened the window of
my imagination, bringing life to the poem,

Bob and Val Henry, models for the wedding garments;

May Irwin and Ruthann Popour, whose editing was a true blessing,

Cindy Van Order and Starr Lichty, who provided opportunities for
choral readings,

And *The English Peasant Smock* by Natalie Hart, copyright 1973,
which provided directions for making the wedding garments,
years ago.

# PREFACE

*"If you extract the precious from the worthless,*
*you become My spokesman," saith the Lord* (Jer. 15:19).

When my husband and I married in 1951, it never occurred to me that our marriage would fall short of our lifetime; consequently, when I was divorced against my will 23 years later, the agony was great. Not only did I feel robbed of a great treasure, but there were eternal consequences for what I did about it. As I struggled to identify what was missing in our marriage, I watched other marriages being rent asunder with increasing frequency. With future generations in mind, I cried out "How can I turn my loss to God's glory? What exactly is the treasure that we lost?"

The answer became clear. The marriage covenant is the treasure we treated as lost. It is the key to family stability, yet we did not fully honor our covenant with God. My husband and I had promised to love each other until death us do part. Neither of us is dead yet; therefore our covenant with God still exists. Even after divorce one must decide whether or not to honor the existing covenant. I have chosen to remain faithful to my vows.

In the decades since our divorce I have tried to teach others about the strengths and blessings of the marriage covenant. Having searched long and hard for words that would adequately quantify this treasure's beauty and worth, at last I found them in the Bible. ***The Beauty of Covenant*** tells the story of a marriage covenant from beginning to end in God's own words.  To God be the glory!

Mary Walmsley

May 2016

# INTRODUCTION

*The Beauty of Covenant* is the story of a marriage covenant from beginning to end presented in the form of a dialogue between a man, a woman, a chorus of people, and God.

As a lifelong chorister I chose to present the concept of Covenant as a choral experience because I find that choral reading or singing adds a new dimension to the text. Also, it can be personally beneficial, even uplifting. In a choir of sopranos, altos, tenors, and bases, my alto voice represents a necessary part of the complete choral sound. I know where I fit in; I blend with the others, and it matters that I hold my part. In like manner, a choral reading of *The Beauty of Covenant* will help each participant identify his or her part in the whole of a covenant with God.

After spending the summer of 1949 with the von Trapp family at their Music Camp in Vermont, I returned in September to help with one of the daughter's wedding. There I first learned of the old European tradition that a bride and bridegroom would wear their wedding garments on the day of the wedding and also for burial, the first and last days of their marriage covenant. With this tradition in mind I chose to create wedding garments fashioned after old English smocks. In days of yore smocks were worn as work garments by men and women alike. Marriage is work, the work of a lifetime. The technique of smocking adds a dimension of elasticity to a garment, in this case allowing for the expansions and contractions of a mortal frame throughout a lifetime; therefore these wedding garments would still fit no matter when one was called 'home.'

The text of this epic poem is almost entirely Scripture. The story is told using words, phrases, and sentences found in both Old and New Testament, whereby the immediacy of God and His Word are enhanced. At the end of each line is a number referring to an end note at the back of the book listing the reference. Approximately 90% of the text is from the Bible; the remaining 10% are my words, as indicated with my initials, MW.

This work was accomplished with the use of an NASB (New American Standard Bible) translation. If the reader chooses to check the references apart from the end notes, I encourage you to use a New American Standard translation of the Bible.

May the Lord God bless your reading and reflections thereon.

Mary Walmsley

*Whoever speaks, let him speak, as it were, the utterances of God; whoever serves, let him do so as by the strength which God supplies; so that in all things God may be glorified through Jesus Christ, to whom belongs the glory and dominion forever and ever. Amen.*

2 Peter 4:11

# TABLE OF CONTENTS

# PART 1

# Courtship

| | | |
|---|---|---|
| LORD - | Stand by the ways and see | 1 |
| | And ask for the ancient paths, | 2 |
| | Where the good way is, and walk in it. | 3 |
| | And you will find rest for your souls. | 4 |
| | | |
| CHORUS - | The ways of a man | 5 |
| | Are before the eyes of the Lord. | 6 |
| | | |
| LORD - | For My eyes are open to all their ways; | 7 |
| | They are not hidden from My face. | 8 |
| | | |
| CHORUS - | There is one thing which is too wonderful for us, | 9 |
| | The way of a man with a maid. | 10 |
| | | |
| MAID - | How handsome you are, and so pleasant! | 11 |
| | Your bright eyes gladden my heart. | 12 |
| | Draw me after you, my beloved, | 13 |
| | And let us run together! | 14 |
| | | |
| MAN - | All my springs of joy are in you, my darling. | 15 |
| | You lift me up to the wind | 16 |
| | And cause me to ride among the clouds | 17 |
| | For the hope that is in me. | 18 |
| | | |
| MAID - | How sweet are thy words to my taste! | 19 |
| | My heart and my flesh sing for joy! | 20 |
| | Blessed be the Lord God who sent you to me this day. | 21 |

MAN -      My delight is in you, my darling!                                22
           You are beautiful of form and face.                             23

CHORUS -   Do not look at the outward appearance,                          24
           But see as God sees,                                            25
               For He looks at the heart.                                  26
           The Lord is a God of knowledge,                                 27
           And with Him actions are weighed.                               28

MAID -     My beloved is set apart as a godly man,                         29
               A righteous man and blameless in our time                   30
                   As he walks with God.                                   31
           In his presence is fullness of joy.                             32

MAN -      My darling, your speech is always with grace;                   33
               Your loveliness is like the flower of the field.            34

MAID -     Do you stare at me because I am pious?                          35

MAN -      I have heard good news of your faith and love,                  36
               That you set your mind on the things above                  37
                   And have faith in the working of God.                   38

MAID -     It is my ambition to lead a quiet life,                         39
               Devoting myself to prayer,                                  40
                   Keeping alert with an attitude of thanksgiving.         41

MAN -      To me, my darling, you are like a corner column                 42
               Fashioned as for a palace,                                  43
                   A pillar of faith in the house of God.                  44
           You stand in the council of the Lord                           45
               To see and hear His word.                                   46
           The joy and gladness in your voice                             47
               Puts gladness in my heart.                                  48

MAID -   My heart rejoices in God                                        49
   Because we both trust in His holy name.                50
I am my beloved's, and his desire is for me.                            51

CHORUS -   Listen, O daughter,                                          52
   Give attention and incline your ear.                  53
Forget your people and your father's house;                            54
   Then your beloved will desire your beauty.            55

MAID -   The word of God is very near,                                  56
   In his mouth and in his heart.                        57
I rejoice to see his good discipline                                   58
   And the stability of his faith in Christ.             59
My beloved is well spoken of by the people;                            60
   He is wholly desirable.                               61

MAN -   My dove, my perfect one, is unique.                            62
   They say, "Who is this that is intelligent           63
    And beautiful in appearance?                    64
   Who abounds with deeds of kindness and charity?"      65
I come to see whether the report was true,                             66
   That her adornment is                                 67
    The hidden person of her heart.                 68
   A gentle and quiet spirit is hers, which is precious. 69
Christ dwells in my beloved's heart through faith,                     70
   Which makes my heart beat faster.                     71

MAID -   My beloved does nothing great or small                       72
   Contrary to the Lord,                                 73
    For the law of our God is in his heart.         74
He disciplines himself for the purpose of godliness,                   75
   Because godliness holds promise                       76
    For the present life                            77
    And also for the life to come.                  78

| | | |
|---|---|---:|
| MAN - | My darling, God created you for my sake; | 79 |
| | You ought to have | 80 |
| | A symbol of authority on your head. | 81 |
| | My heart overflows with a good theme, | 82 |
| | That you encourage my heart. | 83 |
| MAID - | My heart is steadfast, my love! My heart is steadfast! | 84 |
| MAN - | How beautiful is your love, my sister! | 85 |
| | From your heart flow the springs of life. | 86 |
| | Tell me, O you whom my soul loves, | 87 |
| | Why have I found favor in your sight? | 88 |
| CHORUS - | Hear the plan of the Lord which He has planned, | 89 |
| | And His purposes which He has purposed. | 90 |
| | All things are to be done properly | 91 |
| | And in an orderly manner, | 92 |
| | For God is not a God of confusion but of peace. | 93 |
| MAID - | My beloved, I lift up my eyes and see that | 94 |
| | From your shoulders and up | 95 |
| | You are taller than me. | 96 |
| | This is the Lord's doing, | 97 |
| | And it is marvelous in our eyes. | 98 |
| LORD - | Be glad and rejoice forever in what I create. | 99 |
| | As Christ is head of the church, | 100 |
| | So the husband is to be head of the wife. | 101 |
| CHORUS - | Therefore both of you must clothe yourselves | 102 |
| | With humility toward the other, | 103 |
| | For God is opposed to the proud | 104 |
| | But gives grace to the humble. | 105 |

Whoever between you wishes to become great 106
    Shall be the servant, 107
And whoever wishes to be first shall be the slave, 108
    Just as the Son of Man came to serve. 109

MAID - I hear with my ears the sound of my beloved's voice, 110
    That it is louder than mine, 111
This is the Lord's doing; 112
    It is marvelous in our eyes. 113
As spokesman of his household 114
    The voice of authority will be heard. 115

MAN - She who speaks truth tells what is right, 116
    And she who speaks right is loved. 117
Her words are wise and gracious; 118
    The mouth of the righteous flows with wisdom. 119

LORD – Whether it is the man or the woman, 120
    If you extract the precious from the worthless, 121
        You will become My spokesman. 122

CHORUS - The plans of the Lord's heart stand 123
    From generation to generation. 124

MAID- My beloved is stronger than I. 125
    This is the Lord's doing, 126
        And it is marvelous to see. 127
He rises to be an encouragement 128
    And a protection for me; 129
Alert and strong, he will not allow 130
    His house to be broken into. 131

| | | |
|---|---|---:|
| MAN - | By grace my darling is strong in the Lord | 132 |
| | And in the strength of His might. | 133 |
| | With joy I rejoice before God | 134 |
| | On your account, my darling, | 135 |
| | And pray that I may complete | 136 |
| | What is lacking in your faith, | 137 |
| | For you fill up that which is lacking in me. | 138 |
| | | |
| MAID - | May my gifts be a supply for your need, my love, | 139 |
| | And your gifts a supply for my need, | 140 |
| | That there may be equality. | 141 |
| | | |
| CHORUS – | We see that each regards the other | 142 |
| | As more important than himself. | 143 |
| | May they employ their special gifts | 144 |
| | In serving one another as good stewards | 145 |
| | Of the manifold grace of God. | 146 |
| | | |
| LORD - | Surely, just as I intended, so it has happened; | 147 |
| | And just as I have planned, so it will stand. | 148 |
| | | |
| MAN and MAID - | We will sing, yes, we will sing praises! | 149 |
| | We will give thanks to Thee, O Lord. | 150 |
| | For Your loving-kindness is good, | 151 |
| | It is better than life. | 152 |
| | | |
| CHORUS - | God's hands fashioned and made them altogether; | 153 |
| | And God blessed them each one | 154 |
| | With the blessing appropriate to them. | 155 |
| | Unite their hearts, O Lord. | 156 |
| | Give them one heart and one way, | 157 |
| | That they may fear You always | 158 |
| | For their own good, | 159 |
| | And for the good of their children after them. | 160 |

PART 2

Betrothal

| CHORUS - | Behold how they abound in love for one another! | 1 |
| | Their hearts are encouraged, | 2 |
| | Having been knit together in love. | 3 |
| | God has put it in their hearts | 4 |
| | To execute His purpose | 5 |
| | By having a common purpose. | 6 |
| | | |
| BRIDE - | How beautiful is your love, my beloved! | 7 |
| | My affection abounds all the more toward you | 8 |
| | As I remember that you love from a pure heart, | 9 |
| | From a good conscience and a sincere faith. | 10 |
| | | |
| GROOM - | My darling, I love you fervently from the heart, | 11 |
| | I have known you by name, | 12 |
| | And you have found favor in my sight. | 13 |
| | Indeed, I love you as I love my own life. | 14 |
| | My desire is to take you as my wife. | 15 |
| | You will call upon me, and I will answer you; | 16 |
| | I will be with you in trouble; | 17 |
| | I will rescue you and honor you. | 18 |
| | | |
| BRIDE - | My heart is assured that I love you in truth. | 19 |
| | I gladly give you my hand, | 20 |
| | That we may be joined one to another. | 21 |

| | | |
|---|---|---:|
| LORD - | I will betroth you to Me forever; | 22 |
| | Yes, I will betroth you to Me | 23 |
| | In righteousness and in justice, | 24 |
| | In loving-kindness and in compassion. | 25 |
| | And I will betroth you to Me in faithfulness; | 26 |
| | Then you will know the Lord. | 27 |
| | | |
| CHORUS - | She gives to her beloved a pledge of truth, | 28 |
| | A pledge for her with him. | 29 |
| | Be joyful and rejoice for her, | 30 |
| | All you who love her; | 31 |
| | Be exceedingly glad with her, | 32 |
| | For soon she will be married. | 33 |
| | | |
| | Daughter, prepare yourself | 34 |
| | For your husband's household | 35 |
| | According to the word of God the Father | 36 |
| | And according to the word of His Son Jesus. | 37 |
| | | |
| BRIDE - | My heart overflows with a good theme - | 38 |
| | Behold, I will do something new! | 39 |
| | Soon we will speak marriage vows, | 40 |
| | Clothing ourselves with power from on high | 41 |
| | By making a covenant with God. | 42 |
| | I will make garments for both bride and bridegroom, | 43 |
| | That my beloved and I may put on love, | 44 |
| | Which is the perfect bond of unity. | 45 |
| | | |
| CHORUS - | Behold! Her heart is lifted up in wisdom and skill! | 46 |
| | She will make ready for her wedding day, | 47 |
| | The day a stewardship is entrusted to them, | 48 |
| | A covenant to last a lifetime. | 49 |

Bride and groom will be dressed in readiness,                      50
    Wearing garments of testimony                                51
        that adorn the doctrine of God,                    52
That they may be of the same mind                                   53
    Toward one another.                                          54

GROOM - The plan in your heart is like deep water, my love.         55
Draw it out with understanding,                                     56
    That we may qualify to share                                 57
        In the inheritance of the saints.                   58
Your good work will increase                                        59
    Our knowledge of God;                                        60
This will please the Lord better than any gift!                    61

CHORUS - According to the integrity of her heart                    62
    The bride brings forth holy garments                         63
        Wrought in love.                                    64
The Lord will be pleased to establish them                          65
    As a holy people to Himself.                                 66

BRIDE - Are you missing a rib, my beloved?                          67
    For God fashioned me out of one!                             68
I shall cut two garments from the same cloth,                      69
    That we ourselves may appear approved as one.                70
The second will appear similar to the first,                       71
    As though the two had become one;                            72
Yet as star differs from star in glory,                            73
    So your garment will differ from mine,                       74
According to the unique embroidery of each.                        75

| | | |
|---|---|---|
| GROOM - | I am rejoicing over you, my darling! | 76 |
| | Being knit together in love | 77 |
| | And joined to the Lord in a covenant, | 78 |
| | We will be fellow workers | 79 |
| | For the kingdom of God. | 80 |
| | This is the task which God has given us to do, | 81 |
| | With which to occupy ourselves every day. | 82 |
| | For the work of marriage is life and peace, | 83 |
| | Faith and fidelity, hand in hand, | 84 |
| | To serve God shoulder to shoulder. | 85 |
| | | |
| CHORUS - | See how she honors her husband | 86 |
| | By making a cord for his waist, | 87 |
| | That he might gird up his loins like a man | 88 |
| | To fear God as head of his household! | 89 |
| | For as the waistband clings to the waist of a man, | 90 |
| | So the whole household will cling to God. | 91 |
| | | |
| BRIDE - | All this the Lord made me understand. | 92 |
| | As I stitched, His hand was upon me, | 93 |
| | Showing all the details of this pattern. | 94 |
| | | |
| CHORUS - | How well she prepares her way to seek love! | 95 |
| | | |
| GROOM - | I am drawn to you, my darling, my bride. | 96 |
| | For you stand assured in all the will of God. | 97 |
| | I will not keep silent until your righteousness | 98 |
| | Goes forth like brightness, | 99 |
| | And your salvation like a torch that is burning. | 100 |
| | The whole nation will see your righteousness, | 101 |
| | And all the people your glory. | 102 |
| | | |
| BRIDE - | I did not withhold my heart from any pleasure, | 103 |
| | For my heart was pleased because of all my labor. | 104 |

| | | |
|---|---|---|
| CHORUS - | Through the eye of a needle she passes a thread | 105 |
| | Weaving patterns the Lord showed her, | 106 |
| | Yea, even the perfection of beauty, | 107 |
| | A joy for all to see. | 108 |
| | | |
| LORD – | And so you are a blessing, My child. | 109 |
| | Yes, be a blessing, | 110 |
| | And all your family shall be blessed. | 111 |
| | | |
| GROOM – | Isaiah tells us the Lord whistled for the bee, | 112 |
| | And they all came! | 113 |
| | My darling, truly the Lord saved you | 114 |
| | That you might become a blessing. | 115 |
| | I will come and join with you, | 116 |
| | That I, too, may become a blessing; | 117 |
| | For we were called for the very purpose | 118 |
| | That we might be a blessing. | 119 |
| | | |
| BRIDE - | I give thanks to the Lord with all my heart; | 120 |
| | I praise Him among a mighty throng. | 121 |
| | | |
| GROOM - | My darling is a good woman, | 122 |
| | Bringing forth what is good | 123 |
| | From the good treasure of her heart. | 124 |
| | These garments will be a sign of our covenant, | 125 |
| | A memorial for us and for our children | 126 |
| | Before the Lord. | 127 |
| | When they ask, saying, 'What do they mean?' | 128 |
| | Then we shall say to them, | 129 |
| | "The Lord God made a covenant with us," | 130 |
| | That the generations to come might know | 131 |
| | We are joined to one another by God | 132 |
| | Until death do us part. | 133 |

| | | |
|---|---|---|
| BRIDE - | Let the favor of the Lord our God be upon us | 134 |
| | And confirm for us the work of my hands. | 135 |
| | | |
| GROOM - | Yes, Lord, confirm the work of her hands | 136 |
| | As a good steward of the grace of God. | 137 |
| | | |
| CHORUS - | We rejoice greatly in the Lord; | 138 |
| | Our souls exult in our God, | 139 |
| | For He will clothe this covenant couple | 140 |
| | With garments of salvation. | 141 |
| | | |
| GROOM - | My darling, you have wrapped me | 142 |
| | With a robe of righteousness, | 143 |
| | A labor of love and steadfastness of hope, | 144 |
| | Faith working through love! | 145 |
| | The Lord delighted to prosper you, my darling; | 146 |
| | May He reward you with good | 147 |
| | In return for what you have done for me. | 148 |
| | | |
| BRIDE - | I speak to you with confidence, my beloved, | 149 |
| | Since I am persuaded | 150 |
| | That nothing escapes your notice. | 151 |
| | These garments are not | 152 |
| | For our wedding day only, | 153 |
| | But for the end of our lives as well. | 154 |
| | They are to be worn | 155 |
| | On the first and last days of our covenant, | 156 |
| | At the beginning and at its end. | 157 |
| | | |
| GROOM - | The eyes of the Lord will be upon our ways | 158 |
| | All the days of our covenant, | 159 |
| | For it is to Him that we pay our vows. | 160 |
| | These garments will be kept with care | 161 |
| | As a reminder of our vows and obligations. | 162 |

CHORUS - Let us rejoice and be glad                                    163
  And give glory to God!                                     164
   For the bride has made ready for the wedding.        165
 Again let us rejoice and be glad                                 166
  For the bridegroom has blessed his bride                   167
By accepting the work of her hands.                                    168

GROOM - The time of the wedding is soon to come                        169
  When God will make a covenant with them                    170
   That He will not turn away from them,                171
    To do them good.                               172

LORD – I will give them one heart and one way                          173
  That they may fear me always,                              174
 For their own good                                               175
  And for the good of their children after them.             176

The Bridegroom

The Bride

Two Become One

Details in the embroidery of the Bride's shoulder

PART 3

CHORUS - Ascribe to the Lord, O families of the peoples,                1
   Ascribe to the Lord glory and strength.                2
Come, worship the Lord in holy array.                                  3

Listen to the sound heard from afar!                                   4
  Ringing bells declare what is coming;                      5
   The people all know the joyful sound.                6
  "Come to the wedding!" it seems to say.                    7
How lovely is the sound                                                8
  That brings news of happiness!                             9

The wedding is ready,                                                  10
  The hall is filled with guests;                            11
Elders, children and infants are assembled;                           12
  All are dressed in wedding clothes.                        13
Let the bridegroom come out of his room                               14
  And the bride out of her bridal chamber,                   15
   Both donned in beautiful wedding garments.           16
Clothed with honor and majesty,                                        17
  They will enter the sanctuary                              18
   To speak their vows.                                 19

Go forth, daughters, and gaze on the bridegroom                       20
  On this his wedding day,                                   21
   The day of his gladness of heart.                    22

| | | |
|---|---|---|
| GROOM - | I will lead them in procession | 23 |
| | To the house of God | 24 |
| | With the voice of joy and thanksgiving. | 25 |
| | They will be led forth with gladness and rejoicing. | 26 |
| CHORUS - | Lift up your eyes round about and see; | 27 |
| | Behold your bride, my son! | 28 |
| | You will see her and be glad. | 29 |
| | She comes to you in raiment of needlework. | 30 |
| | Can a bride forget her wedding attire? | 31 |
| BRIDE - | I was glad when they said to me, | 32 |
| | "Let us go into the house of the Lord." | 33 |
| CHORUS - | He who now has the bride is the bridegroom. | 34 |
| GROOM - | My darling, | 35 |
| | I am full of gladness with your presence, | 36 |
| | For he who sees me sees the one beside me. | 37 |
| BRIDE - | My beloved, in your presence is fullness of joy, | 38 |
| | Now that you, my lord, are at my right hand, | 39 |
| | I will not be shaken; | 40 |
| | Therefore my heart is glad and my glory rejoices; | 41 |
| | Moreover my flesh abides in hope. | 42 |
| | I am ready to make vows to the Lord our God, | 43 |
| | Binding myself with a binding obligation | 44 |
| | To be your companion and wife by covenant | 45 |
| | As long as we both have life. | 46 |
| GROOM - | We love, my darling, because God first loved us. | 47 |
| | I shall love you as I love myself. | 48 |

The vows which I shall speak today 49
    Are not too difficult for me, 50
        Nor are the words out of reach. 51
They are very near, 52
    In my mouth and in my heart, 53
        That I may keep them. 54

CHORUS - Daughter, dedicate yourself to the Lord today 55
    So that He may bestow blessings upon you. 56
Because your husband is to be your lord, 57
    You will submit to him. 58
Honor the life of your beloved 59
    And the life of his soul, 60
That his soul may be precious in your sight 61
    This day and always. 62

Son, may the soul of your darling 63
    be precious in your sight. 64
As you honor her life and the life of her soul. 65
    May it go well with her because of you, 66
        And may her soul live on account of you. 67

BRIDE & GROOM - Come, let us join ourselves to the Lord 68
    In a covenant that shall not be forgotten. 69
May the Lord be 70
    A true and faithful witness between us 71
If we do not act in accordance with the covenant 72
    Which we make with the Lord our God. 73

*In the Name of God,*

*I, _____, take you, _____,*

*to be my wife*

*to have and to hold*

*from this day forward,*

*for better for worse,*

*for richer for poorer,*

*in sickness and in health,*

*to love and to cherish*

*until we are parted by death.*

*This is my solemn vow.*

*In the Name of God,*

*I, _____, take you, _____,*

*to be my husband*

*to have and to hold*

*from this day forward,*

*for better for worse,*

*for richer for poorer,*

*in sickness and in health,*

*to love and to cherish*

*until we are parted by death.*

*This is my solemn vow.*

CHORUS – The couple stood before the Lord | 76
  To make their covenant; | 77
The people kept silent | 78
  As the man and woman made vows to Him. | 79
Out of the heart each spoke in turn, | 80
  Promising to love as Christ loves us, | 81
And all the people joined in the covenant. | 82

LORD – You have made a covenant | 83
  With Me, your Lord. | 84
Even as the Father is in Me | 85
  And I in the Father, | 86
  I am in your covenant, | 87
   Making a cord of three strands. | 88
What therefore God has joined together, | 89
  Let no man separate. | 90

CHORUS – The Lord has done a great thing! | 91
Know therefore that the Lord your God | 92
Is a faithful God who keeps His covenant | 93
  And His loving-kindness | 94
   With those who love Him. | 95

Bride and groom, | 96
  You may greet one another with a holy kiss. | 97

GROOM – My darling, I have made | 98
  A marriage covenant with you. | 99
   It is a covenant to do us good. | 100
You are now bone of my bones | 101
  And flesh of my flesh. | 102
We, who were two, are now one body | 103
  And individually members one of another. | 104

I will never break my covenant with you;     105
    As the Lord lives and your soul lives,     106
    I will not leave you.     107

BRIDE - My beloved, you have brought me     108
    Into a covenant of the Lord with you,     109
    Therefore the Lord is between us forever.     110
I shall pay the vows which my lips have uttered.     111
    I'll not leave you until I have done     112
    What I have promised.     113

CHORUS - Impress the words of the covenant     114
    On your heart and on your soul;     115
Give heed to yourself     116
    And keep your soul diligently,     117
    So that you do not forget these words.     118
May they not depart from your heart     119
    All the days of your life,     120
But make them known     121
    To your children and to your grandchildren.     122

BRIDE & GROOM - We bow our knees before the Father,     123
    From whom every family     124
    Derives its name.     125

CHORUS - Daughter, you are no longer     126
    A youth in your father's house,     127
No longer shall your name be called     128
    By your father's name.     129
You will now be called by a new name     130
    Which the mouth of the Lord has designated.     131
This will be a sign of your covenant,     132
    That all may know you are his wife.     133

GROOM - My beloved, you are mine, and I am yours.                    134
    My life is bound up in your life;                              135
      What I do have, I give to you.                         136

BRIDE - Gladly will I take my husband's name,                        137
    That we may be one.                                            138

GROOM - My darling, I take pleasure                                  139
    In making you my wife;                                         140
    And so I take this ring from my hand                           141
      And put it on your finger.                             142
    It is a reminder that I have pledged                           143
      My allegiance to you, my wife,                         144
    I am yours and give myself up for you;                         145
      I will love you as I love my own life.                 146

LORD - These are my chosen ones                                      147
    In whom My soul delights.                                      148
    I am the Lord;                                                 149
      I have called you in righteousness;                    150
    I appoint you as a covenant to the people,                     151
      As a light to the nation.                              152
    I am the Lord, that is My name.                                153

BRIDE & GROOM - Having pledged allegiance                            154
    To each other,                                                 155
    We will certainly carry out every word                         156
      That has proceeded from our mouths.                    157

LORD - I will keep you and give you for a covenant                   158
    Of the people, to restore the land.                            159
    Verily I say to you,                                           160
      Be faithful until death,                               161
      And I will give you the crown of life.                 162

And you, O people, are My witnesses,      163
     And I am God.      164

CHORUS - We are witnesses;      165
     We are witnesses of these things.      166
We join with our kinsmen in taking an oath      167
     To walk in God's law,      168
To keep and observe all the commandments      169
     Of God our Lord.      170
Let us regard ourselves as servants of Christ      171
     And stewards of the marriage covenant.      172

BRIDE & GROOM - We must guard through the Holy Spirit      173
     The treasure which has been entrusted to us.      174

CHORUS - Even though it is only a man's covenant,      175
     Yet when it has been ratified,      176
No one sets it aside      177
     Or adds conditions to it.      178
One day we will all stand      179
     Before the judgment seat      180
     And give account of ourselves to God.      181

GROOM - My wife and I shall continually pray      182
     That our faith will supply moral excellence.      183

CHORUS - Be diligent to preserve the unity of the Spirit      184
     In the bond of peace,      185
     Sanctifying Christ as Lord in your hearts.      186
Now may the God of peace Himself      187
     Sanctify you entirely.      188

| | |
|---|---:|
| BRIDE & GROOM - May our spirit and soul and body | 189 |
| Be preserved complete, | 190 |
| Without blame at the coming | 191 |
| Of our Lord Jesus Christ. | 192 |
| | |
| CHORUS - Behold! a wedded couple in priestly apparel, | 193 |
| Fellow-heirs of the grace of life, | 194 |
| Equal in glory and greatness! | 195 |
| The voice of joy and the voice of gladness | 196 |
| Are heard in the land, | 197 |
| The voice of the bridegroom | 198 |
| And the voice of the bride, | 199 |
| The voice of those who say, | 200 |
| "Give thanks to the Lord of hosts, | 201 |
| For the Lord is good, | 202 |
| For His loving-kindness is everlasting." | 203 |

PART 4

# Marriage

CHORUS - Look among our nation! Observe!                    1
     Be astonished! Wonder!                              2
God is doing something in your days -                        3
     You would not believe if you were told.           4
A man and wife are being built up                           5
     As a spiritual house,                             6
A holy priesthood acceptable to God.                        7


HUSBAND - My bride and I have built us a house;             8
     Righteousness and justice are its foundation.     9
The walls are called 'Salvation'                            10
     And the doors 'Praise;'                           11
       Within is the sound of singing.               12
All who enter give greetings of peace.                      13
     How lovely is our dwelling place!                 14


WIFE - A wise man and discerning is my husband,            15
     The builder of an enduring house.                 16
In our house we walk in the integrity of our hearts.        17


CHORUS - The work of righteousness will be peace,          18
     And the service of righteousness,                 19
       Quietness and security.                       20


HUSBAND - The Lord dwells in our midst,                    21
     And we are His fellow workers.                    22

|  | We bring the whole tithe into His storehouse | 23 |
|  | So that He will open for us | 24 |
|  | The windows of heaven | 25 |
|  | And pour out blessings | 26 |
|  | Until it overflows. | 27 |

WIFE - I love the habitation of this house, 28
For surely the Lord is in this place! 29
Our marriage is an enclosed garden 30
In which God placed us. 31
Out of its ground The Lord God will cause 32
Good things to grow. 33

CHORUS - But alas, this man and wife no longer 34
Walk in the newness of marriage; 35
Troubles have come upon them. 36
It is inevitable that stumbling blocks come. 37
Faded flowers have appeared in the garden; 38
The time has arrived for pruning the vines. 39
They must work the works of marriage, 40
In order to honor God and 41
Keep the covenant they made with Him. 42

WIFE - Why are you in despair, O my soul? 43
And why are you disturbed within me? 44

HUSBAND - My ear tests words as the palate tastes food. 45
Why are you troubled, my love? 46
Have I given cause for offense in something? 47

WIFE - Beloved husband, I find a hurtful way in you. 48
I pour out my complaint before you. 49
Strife has come between you and me. 50

Offenses are piling in heaps,      51
    Making our marriage become foul.      52

CHORUS - Since no temptation has overtaken you      53
    But such as is common to man,      54
We exhort you as man and wife,      55
    That you both agree      56
        To let no division be between you.      57
May this valley of trouble become a door of hope.      58

HUSBAND - If I despise the claim of my darling      59
    When she files a complaint against me,      60
What then could I do when God arises?      61
    When He calls me to account,      62
        What will I answer Him?      63
No, if my darling has something against me,      64
    Before the sun goes down      65
        I shall go and be reconciled to her.      66
For love bears all things, believes all things,      67
    Hopes all things, endures all things.      68
        Love never fails.      69

LORD - The mountains may be removed,      70
    And the hills may shake,      71
But My loving-kindness      72
    Will not be removed from you;      73
        My covenant of peace will not be shaken.      74

HUSBAND - Arise, my darling, my beautiful one,      75
    And come along.      76
Since your soul is troubled within you,      77
    Let us be restored to each other in private.      78

God has been a witness between me and you; 79
He is greater than our heart 80
And knows all things. 81

WIFE - Let us be reconciled and make friends quickly. 82
Let us confess our sins to each other 83
And pray for each other, 84
That we may be healed. 85

HUSBAND - My darling, I have heard your complaint. 86
I have sinned greatly in what I have done. 87
Please forgive my sin, for I did wrong. 88
Take away the iniquity of your loving husband; 89
I will not offend you any more. 90

WIFE - My dear beloved, 91
I no longer count your trespasses against you. 92
Also, I make mention today of my own offenses. 93

HUSBAND - Just as the Lord has forgiven me, 94
So do I forgive you. 95

CHORUS - In the far corner of the garden 96
Is a pile of dead leaves; 97
Trodden down in the water of the manure pile, 98
They decay like a rotten thing. 99
In time they become a heap of fertile soil 100
From which new shoots will sprout, 101
To show the meaning of 102
Rising from the dead. 103

HUSBAND - Let us put the matter of our offenses 104
   On the compost heap, 105
  That our love may be fervent again, 106
   For love covers a multitude of sins. 107

CHORUS - God has given us the ministry of reconciliation 108
   That the sins previously committed 109
    Will be forgiven, 110
  That love may be restored, 111
   Which is the perfect bond of unity. 112

HUSBAND - As the rain and the snow 113
   Come down from heaven 114
  And do not return without watering the earth 115
   And making it bear and sprout, 116
  So may my tears fall onto our compost heap, 117
   Causing new shoots to sprout, 118
    Renewing life for this covenant couple. 119

CHORUS - Drip down, O tears of repentance, 120
   Like clouds pouring down righteousness, 121
  That the earth might open up 122
   And salvation bear fruit, 123
    And righteousness spring up with it. 124
  Cleanse your conscience from dead works 125
   To serve the living God. 126
  The God of grace will Himself perfect, 127
   Confirm, strengthen, and establish you. 128

HUSBAND - God leads us in triumph in Christ; 129
   He manifests through us the sweet aroma 130
    Of the knowledge of Him in every place ... 131

WIFE - . . . That we may be a fragrance of Christ to God. 132

CHORUS - As you previously began the work of marriage, 133
May you complete this gracious work as well, 134
Proving the sincerity of your love. 135
You first began years ago not only to do this, 136
But also to desire to do it. 137
But now finish doing it also, that 138
Just as there was the readiness to desire it, 139
So may there also be 140
completion by your ability. 141

HUSBAND - I cherish you, my darling, my bride, 142
Because we are members of Christ's body 143
And share sweet fellowship together. 144

WIFE - And you, my beloved,  are a comforter, 145
One who restores my soul; 146
You are the help of my countenance, 147
My companion and friend. 148

CHORUS - They walk in a manner worthy of the God 149
Who calls us 150
Into His own kingdom and glory. 151
With souls purified through obedience to the truth, 152
They sustain each other with a willing spirit. 153

HUSBAND - My darling, I am humbled by the vows we made; 154
You submit yourself to me 155
As is fitting in the Lord. 156
And you do your work heartily, my darling, 157
As for the Lord rather than for me, 158
Knowing that from the Lord you will receive 159
The reward of the inheritance. 160

WIFE -    We took an oath that we would do          161
            According to our promise.                 162
        I am comforted about you                     163
            through your faith, my love,             164
        For you act like a strong man               165
            Standing firm in the Lord.               166

HUSBAND - My darling, you are my crown!              167

CHORUS - Their mouth is filled with laughter as they say,   168
            "The Lord has done great things for us."  169

HUSBAND AND WIFE - The Lord has done great things for us,   170
            And we are glad!                          171

CHORUS - Go your way until the end of your life;     172
            Then you will enter into rest             173
        And rise again for your allotted portion      174
            At the end of the age.                     175

PART 5

## Reward

CHORUS - Those who wait for the Lord                    1
    Will gain new strength.                          2
They will mount up with wings like eagles.              3
    They will run and not get tired;                4
They will walk and not become weary.                    5

Who is this coming from the distance,                   6
    Leaning on her beloved?                         7
Come near, come near,                                   8
    That we may gaze at you!                        9
Those who see you ponder over you, saying,              10
    "Are these the elders of the land               11
Renowned for being sound in faith,                      12
    In love and in perseverance?"                  13

HUSBAND - Why should you gaze at us                     14
    As at the dance of two old people?              15
God has crowned us both                                 16
    With love and compassion.                      17
Our years have been satisfied with good things          18
    So that our youth is renewed like the eagle!   19

WIFE - We are advanced in years and rich toward God.    20
    We do not boast beyond our measure             21
        But with the hope that our faith will grow.  22
My beloved is as strong today                           23
    As he was when first married.                  24

HUSBAND - My darling does not consider 25
  The years of her life 26
  Because God keeps her occupied 27
   With the gladness of her heart. 28

CHORUS - Behold, the Lord will come with might; 29
  His reward is with him 30
   And His recompense before Him. 31
  Truly the day of the Lord is coming, 32
   When each one of us shall give account 33
   Of himself to God. 34

  Husband and wife, what will you say to Him? 35

HUSBAND and WIFE - We will say to our God, 36
  The great and awesome God, 37
   Who dost keep covenant and loving-kindness, 38
  "Do not let all the hardship 39
   Seem insignificant before You, 40
  Which has occurred to us 41
   From the day of our marriage to this day. 42
  You are just in all that has come upon us, 43
   For You have dealt faithfully 44
   When we acted wickedly." 45

HUSBAND - Had it not been the Lord who was on my side 46
  When temptation tried to overtake me, 47
   I would have destroyed myself. 48
  Blessed be the Lord who has not given us 49
   To be enticed by our own lust, 50
  For He knows how to rescue 51
   The godly from temptation. 52

CHORUS - This man has kept the ways of the Lord;                          53
    By faith he refused to commit adultery,                          54
      Choosing rather to keep his covenant.                          55
He considered the reward of eternal life                          56
    Greater riches than the enjoyment                          57
      Of the passing pleasures of sin.                          58
By faith he endured,                          59
    As seeing Him who is unseen.                          60

WIFE - If the Lord had not been my help,                          61
    When I was tempted by the devil,                          62
My soul would soon have dwelt                          63
    In the abode of silence;                          64
But I resisted the devil,                          65
    And he fled.                          66
My soul escaped as a bird                          67
    Out of the snare of the trapper;                          68
The snare was broken,                          69
    And we have escaped.                          70

HUSBAND and WIFE - Blessed be the Lord,                          71
    Who bound us with Him by covenant.                          72
God is good and does good;                          73
    He tests us to do good for us in the end.                          74

CHORUS - The fear of the Lord is the beginning of wisdom;                          75
    How blessed are the husband and wife                          76
      Who fear the Lord and walk in His ways.                          77
This elder with his chosen lady,                          78
    Whom we love in truth,                          79
      Are teaching what is good.                          80
They walk in a manner worthy of the Lord,                          81
    To please Him in all respects.                          82

| | | |
|---|---|---:|
| HUSBAND | According to the riches of God's grace | 83 |
| | We have forgiveness of our trespasses; | 84 |
| | Therefore we still walk in love, | 85 |
| | Just as Christ also loved us | 86 |
| | And gave Himself up for us. | 87 |
| | | |
| | Let us bless our God, my darling; | 88 |
| | Let us sound His praise abroad, | 89 |
| | For He keeps us in life. | 90 |
| | | |
| WIFE - | Bless the Lord, O my soul, | 91 |
| | And all that is within me, bless His Holy name. | 92 |
| | | |
| HUSBAND and WIFE - | Bless the Lord, O my soul, | 93 |
| | And forget none of His benefits. | 94 |
| | | |
| CHORUS - | Many couples wish to see | 95 |
| | The things which you have seen | 96 |
| | And do not see them; | 97 |
| | They wish to hear the things which you hear | 98 |
| | And do not hear them. | 99 |
| | You are greatly esteemed in all the land, | 100 |
| | Receiving respectful greetings in the market. | 101 |
| | | |
| HUSBAND and WIFE - | We have done | 102 |
| | Only that which we ought to have done. | 103 |
| | | |
| LORD - | Behold, the time for you to die is near. | 104 |
| | | |
| HUSBAND - | The end of our marriage is nigh. | 105 |
| | May we have proved what the will of God is, | 106 |
| | That which is good | 107 |
| | And acceptable and perfect. | 108 |

CHORUS - Prepare to meet your God,                                    109
         O Husband and Wife.                          110
We know your readiness,                                               111
    That you have been preparing                    112
       Since the day of your wedding.          113
We pray that our boasting about you                                  114
    May not be empty,                               115
But that you may be prepared                                         116
    For the previously promised bountiful gift.     117

HUSBAND - By faith my darling,                                       118
    Being warned about things not yet seen,         119
In reverence prepared garments of salvation                          120
    For the salvation of our household.             121
Surely she will become                                               122
    An heir of the righteousness                    123
       Which is according to faith!             124

WIFE - Let us fear while a promise remains                           125
    Of entering His rest,                           126
Lest either of us                                                    127
    Should seem to have come short of it.            128

CHORUS - Have confidence when He appears,                            129
    And do not shrink away from Him                 130
      In shame at His coming.                 131
God will gather His godly ones to Himself,                           132
    Those who made a covenant with Him               133
      By sacrifice.                           134

HUSBAND and WIFE: Our soul waits for the Lord.                       135

43

CHORUS - It is appointed for men to die once,          136
      And after this comes judgment.       137
The Lord has fixed a day in which        138
      He will judge the world in righteousness.   139

This husband and wife have died;        140
      The days of their marriage are now fulfilled.  141
The promises have come to an end;      142
      The vows are accomplished.     143
         Their marriage covenant is now valid.  144
Someone else will gird them        145
      In their wedding garments     146
And lay their bodies in their own grave,   147
      Clothed with garments of salvation!  148
Now is the appointed day        149
      When the husband and wife come   150
         And present themselves before the Lord.  151
They come to God believing that He is,  152
      That He is a rewarder     153
         Of those who seek Him.    154

HUSBAND - I stand at the door of God the Father's house,  155
      The place Jesus has prepared for me.  156

CHORUS - Behold, the Judge is standing right at the door!  157

HUSBAND - I knock at His door, saying,    158
      "Lord, open up to us!     159
Open to us the gates of righteousness,  160
      That we may enter through them  161
      And give thanks to the Lord."  162

| | | |
|---|---|---|
| WIFE - | While my beloved is knocking, | 163 |
| | Our hearts are melting | 164 |
| | And our knees are knocking, | 165 |
| | Lest there be in either of us an unbelieving heart | 166 |
| | That falls away from the living God. | 167 |
| | | |
| CHORUS – | O, you of anxious heart, | 168 |
| | Take courage, fear not. | 169 |
| | In every nation, the man who fears Him | 170 |
| | And does what is right | 171 |
| | Is welcome to Him. | 172 |
| | | |
| | Immediately the door opens | 173 |
| | To them who had come knocking. | 174 |
| | | |
| HUSBAND and WIFE - | My Lord and my God! | 175 |
| | | |
| HUSBAND - | This is the Lord for whom we have waited, | 176 |
| | That He might save us! | 177 |
| | | |
| WIFE - | Let us rejoice and be glad! | 178 |
| | | |
| LORD - | Come now, and let us reason together. | 179 |
| | Though your sins are as scarlet, | 180 |
| | They will be as white as snow. | 181 |
| | My reward is with Me | 182 |
| | To render to every man | 183 |
| | According to what he has done. | 184 |
| | | |
| CHORUS - | Today they will give account to Him who is ready | 185 |
| | To judge the living and the dead. | 186 |
| | They shall render account | 187 |
| | For every careless word they have spoken. | 188 |

| | | |
|---|---|---|
| LORD - | Present your case. | 189 |
| | Bring forward your strong arguments, | 190 |
| | That you may be proved right. | 191 |
| | By your own words I will judge you. | 192 |

| | | |
|---|---|---|
| HUSBAND and WIFE - | We have sinned | 193 |
| | And fallen short of the glory of God; | 194 |
| | Yet we repented and returned | 195 |
| | So that our sins might be wiped away, | 196 |
| | In order that times of refreshing | 197 |
| | Might come in Your presence, O Lord. | 198 |

| | | |
|---|---|---|
| LORD - | Surely, just as I have intended, | 199 |
| | So it has happened. | 200 |
| | My law has been written on your hearts; | 201 |
| | I have been your God, | 202 |
| | And you have been My people. | 203 |

| | | |
|---|---|---|
| HUSBAND and WIFE - | Thou hast tried us, O God; | 204 |
| | Yet Thou didst bring us out | 205 |
| | Into a place of abundance. | 206 |
| | We have come to know and have believed | 207 |
| | The love which You have for us. | 208 |

| | | |
|---|---|---|
| LORD - | You have indeed obeyed My voice | 209 |
| | And kept My covenant, | 210 |
| | You are My own special treasure | 211 |
| | Among all peoples. | 212 |
| | You have done the will of My Father | 213 |
| | Who is in heaven. | 214 |
| | Well done, good and faithful servants; | 215 |
| | Enter the kingdom of heaven | 216 |
| | And into the joy of your Lord! | 217 |
| | Come! Be with Me in Paradise. | 218 |

CHORUS - The Lord reaches out His hand,          219
      And brings them into the house with Him.      220
    Shout for joy, O son and daughter!      221
      Rejoice and exult with all your heart,      222
    For the Lord has taken away      223
      His judgment against you.      224
    He will exult over you with joy;      225
      He will rejoice over you with shouts of joy.      226

HUSBAND and WIFE - We rejoice greatly in the Lord,      227
      And our soul exults in our God;      228
    For He has clothed us with garments of salvation      229
      And wrapped us with a robe of righteousness.      230

CHORUS - You have, indeed, entered into His joy!      231
      You have left the beauty of your covenant      232
        As an inheritance to your children forever!      233
    Let us tell it to the next generation,      234
      That the generation to come might know,      235
    Even the children yet to be born,      236
      That they may rise and tell it to their children,      237
    For this man and wife glorified God on the earth,      238
      Having accomplished the work of marriage      239
        Which He had given them to do.      240

LORD – I, the Lord God, set eternity in their hearts,      241
      And by faith they gained approval.      242
    They served My purpose      243
      In their own generation      244
        By holding marriage in honor,      245
    The unchanging love to which they did swear      246
      On the day of their wedding.      247

These are my beloved children                                     248
    With whom I am well pleased!                             249

CHORUS - And all the people answered and said, "Amen!"            250

# 1–4  Thus says the Lord,
     "Stand by the ways and see and ask for the ancient paths,
     Where the good way is, and walk in it;
     And you shall find rest for your souls" - Jer. 6:16.

# 5-6  The ways of a man are before the eyes of the Lord - Pr. 5:21.

# 7–8  "For My eyes are on all their ways;
     They are not hidden from My face" - Jer. 16:17.

# 9  There are three things which are too wonderful for me
     - Pr. 30:18.

# 10  And the way of a man with a maid - Pr. 30:19.

# 11  "How handsome you are my beloved, and so pleasant!"
     - SS 1:16.

# 12  Bright eyes gladden the heart. - Pr. 15:30.

# 13-14  "Draw me after you and let us run together!" - SS 1:4.

# 15  "All my springs of joy are in you" - Ps. 87:7.

# 16-17  "Thou dost lift me up to the wind and cause me to ride"
     - Job 30:22.

# 18  MW

# 19  How sweet are Thy words to my taste! - Ps. 119:103.

| | |
|---|---|
| # 20 | My heart and my flesh sing for joy to the living God - Ps. 84:2. |
| # 21 | "Blessed be the Lord God of Israel, who sent you this day to meet me" - 1 Sam. 25:32. |
| # 22 | For the Lord delights in you - Is. 62:4. |
| # 23 | Rachel was beautiful of form and face - Gen. 29:17. |
| # 24-26 | "Do not look at his appearance or at the height of his stature . . . for God sees not as man sees . . . but the Lord looks at the heart" - 1 Sam. 16:7. |
| # 27–28 | "For the Lord is a God of knowledge, And with Him actions are weighed" - 1 Sam. 2:3. |
| # 29 | But know that the Lord has set apart the godly man for Himself - Ps. 4:3. |
| # 30 | Noah was a righteous man, blameless in his time - Gen. 6:9. |
| # 31 | MW |
| # 32 | In Thy presence is fullness of joy - P. 16:11. |
| # 33 | Let your speech always be with grace - Col. 4:6. |
| # 34 | All flesh is grass, and all its loveliness is like the flower of the field - Is. 40:6. |
| # 35 | "Do not stare at me because I am swarthy" - SS 1:6. |
| # 36 | Timothy has come to us from you, and has brought us good news of your faith and love - 1 Th. 3:6. |
| # 37 | Set your mind on things above, not on the things that are on earth - Col. 3:2. |

# 38     You were also raised up with Him through faith in the working of God - Col. 2:12.

# 39     Make it your ambition to lead a quiet life - 1 Th. 4:11.

# 40 - 41     Devote yourselves to prayer, keeping alert in it with an attitude of thanksgiving - Col. 4:2.

# 42- 43     [Let] our daughters [be] as corner pillars fashioned as for a palace - Ps. 144:12.

# 44     MW

# 45 - 46     But who has stood in the council of the Lord, That he should see and hear His word? - Jer. 23:18.

# 47     Make me to hear joy and gladness - Ps. 51:8.

# 48     Thou hast put gladness in my heart - Ps. 4:7.

# 49 - 50     For our heart rejoices in Him, Because we trust in His holy name - Ps. 33:21.

# 51     "I am my beloved's, and his desire is for me" - SS 7:10.

# 52 - 55     Listen, O daughter, give attention and incline your ear; Forget your people and your father's house; Then the King will desire your beauty - Ps. 45:10-11.

# 56-57     "But the word is very near you, in your mouth and in your heart, that you may observe it" - Deu. 30:14.

# 58-59     Nevertheless I am with you in spirit, rejoicing to see your good discipline and the stability of your faith in Christ - Col. 2:5.

# 60      A righteous and God-fearing man well spoken of by the entire nation – Ac. 10:22.

# 61      "He is wholly desirable" – SS 5:16.

# 62      "But my dove, my perfect one, is unique" - SS. 6:9.

# 63- 64      The woman was intelligent and beautiful in appearance - 1 Sam. 25:3.

# 65      This woman was abounding with deeds of kindness and charity, which she continually did - Ac. 9:36.

# 66      However, they did not all heed the glad tidings; for Isaiah says, "Lord, who has believed our report?" - Rom. 10:16.

# 67      Let not your adornment be merely external - 1 Pet. 3:3.

# 68 - 69      But let it be the hidden person of the heart, with the imperishable quality of a gentle and quiet spirit, which is precious in the sight of God - 1 Pet. 3:4.

# 70      So that Christ may dwell in your hearts through faith - Eph. 3:17.

# 71      "You have made my heart beat faster, my sister, my bride" - SS 4:9.

# 72 - 73      "I could not do anything, either small or great, contrary to the command of the Lord my God" - Num. 22:18.

# 74      The law of his God is in his heart - Ps. 37:31.

# 75      On the other hand, discipline yourself for the purpose of godliness - 1 Tim. 4:7.

# 76-78    But godliness is profitable for all things, since it holds promise for the present life and also for the life to come  - 1 Tim. 4:8.

# 79    Man was not created for the woman's sake, but woman for the man's sake - 1 Cor. 11:9.

# 80-81    Therefore the woman ought to have a symbol of authority on her head - 1 Cor. 11:10.

# 82    My heart overflows with a good theme - Ps. 45:1.

# 83    And that he may encourage your hearts - Col. 4:8.

# 84    My heart is steadfast, O God, my heart is steadfast - Ps. 57:7.

# 85    "How beautiful is your love my sister, my bride!" - SS. 4:10.

# 86    Watch over your heart with all diligence,
For from it flow the springs of life - Pr. 4:23.

# 87    I sought him whom my soul loves - SS. 3:1.

# 88    "Why have I found favor in your sight that you should take notice of me?" - Ru. 2:10.

# 89-90    Therefore hear the plan of the Lord which He has planned . . . And His purposes which He has purposed - Jer. 49:20.

# 91-92    But let all things be done properly and in an orderly manner - 1 Cor. 14:40.

# 93    For God is not a God of confusion but of peace - 1 Cor. 14:33.

# 94    To Thee I lift up my eyes - Ps. 123:1.

# 95-96     From his shoulders and up he was taller than any of the people - 1 Sam. 9:2.

# 97-98     This is the Lord's doing;
It is marvelous in our eyes - Ps. 118:23.

# 99     "But be glad and rejoice forever in what I create" - Is. 65:18.

# 100-101     For the husband is the head of the wife, as Christ also is the head of the church - Eph. 5:23.

# 102-105     Clothe yourselves with humility toward one another, for God is opposed to the proud, but gives grace to the humble - 1 Pet. 5:5.

# 106-107     "Whoever wishes to become great among you shall be your servant" - Mt. 20:26.

# 108     "Whoever wishes to be first among you shall be your slave" - Mt. 20:27.

# 109     "Just as the Son of Man did not come to be served, but to serve" - Mt. 20:28.

# 110     O God, we have heard with our ears - Ps. 44:1.

# 111     MW

# 112-113     This is the Lord's doing;
It is marvelous in our eyes - Ps. 118:23.

# 114     MW

# 115     And the Lord will cause His voice of authority to be heard - Is. 30:30.

# 116     He who speaks truth tells what is right - Pr. 12:17.

# 117     And he who speaks right is loved - Pr. 16:13.

# 118     Words from the mouth of a wise man are gracious
          – Eccl. 10:12.

# 119     The mouth of the righteous flows with wisdom - Pr. 10:31.

# 120     MW

# 121-122   "And if you extract the precious from the worthless,
          You will become My spokesman" - Jer. 15:19.

# 123-124   The counsel of the Lord stands forever,
          The plans of His heart from generation to generation
          - Ps. 33:11.

# 125     MW

# 126-127   This is the Lord's doing;
          It is marvelous in our eyes - Ps. 118:23.

# 128-129   "I arose to be an encouragement and a protection for
          him" - Dan. 11:1.

# 130-131   "But be sure of this, that if the head of the house had
          known at what time of the night the thief was coming, he
          would have been on the alert and would not have allowed
          his house to be broken into" - Mt. 24:43.

# 132-133   Finally, be strong in the Lord, and in the strength of His
          might - Eph. 6:10.

# 134-135   For what thanks can we render to God for you in return for all the joy with which we rejoice before our God on your account - 1 Th. 3:9.

# 136-137   As we night and day keep praying most earnestly that we may see your face and may complete what is lacking in your faith? - 1 Th. 3:10.

# 138   Now I rejoice . . . in filling up that which is lacking in Christ's afflictions - Col. 1:24.

# 139-141   At this present time your abundance being a supply for their want, that their abundance also may become a supply for your want, that there may be equality - 2 Cor. 8:14.

# 142-143   With humility of mind let each of you regard one another as more important than himself - Phil. 2:3.

# 144-146   As each one has received a special gift, employ it in serving one another, as good stewards of the manifold grace of God - 1 P 4:10.

# 147-148   The Lord of hosts has sworn saying, "Surely, just as I have intended so it has happened, and just as I have planned so it will stand" - Is. 14:24.

# 149   I will sing, yes, I will sing praises to the Lord - Ps. 27:6.

# 150   I will give thanks to Thee, O Lord, among the peoples - Ps. 57:9.

# 151   Answer me, O Lord, for Thy lovingkindness is good - Ps. 69:16.

# 152   Because Thy lovingkindness is better than life - Ps. 63:3.

# 153     "Thy hands fashioned and made me altogether" - Job. 10:8.

# 154-155  He blessed them, every one with the blessing appropriate to him - Gen. 49:28.

# 156     Unite my heart to fear Thy name - Ps. 86:11.

# 157-160  "I will give them one heart and one way, that they may fear Me always, for their own good, and for the good of their children after them" - Jer. 32:39.

# 1    And may the Lord cause you to increase and abound in love for one another - 1 Th. 3:12.

# 2-3    That their hearts may be encouraged, having been knit together in love - Col. 2:2.

# 4-6    "For God has put it in their hearts to execute His purpose by having a common purpose" - Rev. 17:17.

# 7    "How beautiful is your love, my sister, my bride!" - SS 4:10.

# 8    And his affection abounds all the more toward you as he remembers . . . - 2 Cor. 7:15.

# 9-10    But the goal of our instruction is love from a pure heart and a good conscience and a sincere faith - 1 Tim. 1:5.

# 11    Fervently love one another from the heart - 1 Pet. 1:22.

# 12-13    "For you have found favor in My sight, and I have known you by name" - Ex. 33:17.

# 14    Nevertheless let each individual among you also love his own wife even as himself - Eph. 5:33.

# 15    Now Esau saw that Isaac had blessed Jacob and sent him away to Paddan-aram to take to himself a wife from there - Gen. 28:6.

# 16-18    "He will call upon Me, and I will answer him;
I will be with him in trouble;
I will rescue him, and honor him" - Ps. 91:15.

# 19    We shall know by this that we are of the truth, and shall assure our heart before Him - 1 Jn. 3:19.

# 20    MW

# 21    "What God has joined together, let no man separate" - Mt. 19:6.

# 22-27    "And I will betroth you to Me forever;
Yes, I will betroth you to Me
In righteousness and in justice,
In lovingkindness and in compassion;
And I will betroth you to Me in faithfulness.
Then you will know the Lord" - Hos. 2:19-20.

# 28    "Now therefore, please swear to me by the Lord . . . .
And give me a pledge of truth" - Josh. 2:12.

# 29    "Lay down, now, a pledge for me with Thyself" - Job 17:3.

# 30-32    "Be joyful with Jerusalem and rejoice for her,
All you who love her;
Be exceedingly glad for her" - Is. 66:10.

# 33    MW

# 34-35    "And prepare yourselves by your fathers' households in your divisions, according to the writing of David king of Israel" - 2 Chr. 35:4.

# 36-37    MW

# 38 My heart overflows with a good theme - Ps. 45:1.

# 39 "Behold, I will do something new" - Is. 43:19.

# 40-41 MW

# 42 "The Lord our God made a covenant with us at Horeb" - Deu. 5:2.

# 43 MW

# 44-45 And beyond all these things put on love, which is the perfect bond of unity - Col. 3:14.

# 46 MW

# 47 "His bride has made herself ready" - Rev. 19:7.

# 48 I have a stewardship entrusted to me - 1 Cor. 9:17.

# 49 A wife is bound as long as her husband lives - 1 Cor. 7:39.

# 50 "Be dressed in readiness" - Lu. 12:35.

# 51 MW

# 52 Showing all good faith that they may adorn the doctrine of God our Savior in every respect - Tit. 2:10.

# 53-54 Be of the same mind toward one another - Rom. 12:16.

# 55-56 A plan in the heart of a man is like deep water - Pr. 20:5.

# 57-58 Who has qualified us to share in the inheritance of the saints in light - Col. 1:12.

# 59-60      Bearing fruit in every good work and increasing in the knowledge of God - Col. 1:10.

# 61      MW

# 62      "In the integrity of my heart...I have done this" - Gen. 20:5.

# 63      "And they shall make holy garments" - Ex. 28:4.

# 64      MW

# 65-66      "The Lord will establish you as a holy people to Himself" - Deu. 28:9.

# 67-68      And the Lord God fashioned into a woman the rib which He had taken from the man - Gen. 2:22.

# 69      MW

# 70      Just as we have been approved by God to be entrusted with the gospel - 1 Th. 2:4.

# 71      MW

# 72      "A man shall cleave to his wife, and the two shall become one flesh" - Mt. 19:5.

# 73      There is one glory of the sun, and another glory of the moon, and another glory of the stars; for star differs from star in glory - 1 Cor. 15:41.

# 74-75      MW

# 76      I am rejoicing over you - Rom. 16:19.

# 77        That their hearts may be encouraged, having been knit together
            in love - Col. 2:2.

# 78        They will come that they may join themselves to the Lord in an
            everlasting covenant - Jer. 50:5.

# 79-80     Fellow workers for the kingdom of God - Col. 4:11.

# 81-82     I have seen the task which God has given the sons of men
            with which to occupy themselves - Eccl. 3:10.

# 83-84     MW

# 85        To serve Him shoulder to shoulder - Zeph. 3:9.

# 86-87     MW

# 88        "Now gird up your loins like a man" - Job 38:3.

# 89        MW

# 90-91     "For as the waistband clings to the waist of a man, so I made the
            whole household of Israel and the whole household of Judah cling
            to Me," declares the Lord, "that they might be for Me a people for
            renown, for praise and for glory" - Jer. 13:11.

# 92-94     "The Lord made me understand in writing by His hand
            upon me, all the details of this pattern" - 1 Chr. 28:19.

# 95        "How well you prepare our way to seek love!" - Jer. 2:33.

# 96        "I have drawn you with loving-kindness" - Jer. 31:3.

# 97      That you may stand perfect and fully assured in all the will of God - Col. 4:12.

# 98-102    I will not keep quiet until her righteousness goes forth like brightness, and her salvation like a torch that is burning. And the nations will see your righteousness, and all kings your glory - Is. 62:1-2.

# 103-4    I did not withhold my heart from any pleasure, for my heart was pleased because of all my labor - Eccl. 2:10.

# 105      MW

# 106      According to the pattern which the Lord had showed Moses, so he made the lamp stand - Nu. 8:4.

# 107-108   "The perfection of beauty, a joy to all the earth" - Lam. 2:15.

# 109-110   "I will bless you, and make your name great, and so you shall be a blessing" - Gen. 12:2.

# 111      "And in you all the families of the earth shall be blessed" - Gen. 12:3.

# 112-113   "And it will come about in that day, that the Lord will whistle for the fly . . . and they will all come" - Is. 7:18, 19.

# 114-15   "So I will save you that you may become a blessing" - Zech. 8:13.

# 116      MW

# 117      "That you may become a blessing" - Zech. 8:13.

\# 118-119   For you were called for the very purpose that you might inherit a blessing - 1 Pet. 3:9.

\# 120   I will give thanks to the Lord with all my heart - Ps. 111:1.

\# 121   I will praise Thee among a mighty throng - Ps. 35:18.

\# 122-124   "The good man out of the good treasure of his heart brings forth what is good" - Lu. 6:45.

\# 125   "This is the sign of the covenant" - Gen. 9:12.

\# 126-127   That it may be a memorial for the sons of Israel before the Lord - Ex. 30:16.

\# 128-129   "When your children ask later, saying, 'What do these stones mean to you?' then you shall say to them..." - Josh. 4:6-7.

\# 130   "The Lord our God made a covenant with us" - Deu. 5:2.

\# 131   That the generation to come might know, even the children yet to be born - Ps. 78:6.

\# 132   "Consequently they are no longer two, but one flesh. What therefore God has joined together, let no man separate" - Mt. 19:6.

\# 133   MW

\# 134-136   And let the favor of the Lord our God be upon us; And do confirm for us the work of our hands; Yes, confirm the work of our hands. - Ps. 90:17.

\# 137   As each one has received a special gift, employ it in serving one another, as good stewards of the manifold grace of God - 1 Pet. 4:10.

# 138-143  I will rejoice greatly in the Lord,
My soul will exult in my God;
For He has clothed me with garments of salvation,
He has wrapped me with a robe of righteousness - Is. 61:10.

# 144  Constantly bearing in mind your work of faith and labor of love and steadfastness of hope in our Lord Jesus Christ - 1 Th. 1:3.

# 145  But faith working through love - Gal. 5:6.

# 146  "The Lord delighted over you to prosper you" - Deu. 28:63.

# 147-148  "May the Lord therefore reward you with good in return for what you have done to me this day" - 1 Sam. 24:19.

# 149-151  "I speak to him also with confidence, since I am persuaded that none of these things escape his notice" - Ac. 26:26

# 152-157  MW

# 158  For the ways of a man are before the eyes of the Lord, and He watches all his paths - Pr. 5:21.

# 159  MW

# 160  And pay your vows to the Most High - Ps. 50:14.

# 161-162  MW

# 163-165  "Let us rejoice and be glad and give the glory to Him, for the marriage of the Lamb has come and His bride has made herself ready" - Rev. 19:7.

# 166      "Let us rejoice and be glad" - Rev. 19:7.

# 167-168  "O Lord, bless his substance
And accept the work of his hands" - Deu. 33:11.

# 169      MW

# 170-172  "And I will make an everlasting covenant with them that I will not turn away from them, to do them good"
- Jer. 32:40.

# 173-176  "I will give them one heart and one way, that they may fear Me always, for their own good, and for the good of their children after them" - Jer. 32:39.

# 1-3     Ascribe to the Lord, O families of the peoples
          Ascribe to the Lord glory and strength;
          Worship the Lord in holy array - 1 Chr. 16:28-9.

# 4       MW

# 5       Let them bring forth and declare to us what is going to take
          place - Is. 41:22.

# 6       How blessed are the people who know the joyful sound!
          - Ps. 89:15.

# 7       "Come to the wedding feast" - Mt. 22:4.

# 8-9     How lovely on the mountains
          Are the feet of him who brings good news - Is. 52:7.

# 10      Then he said to his slaves, "The wedding is ready" - Mt. 22:8.

# 11      The wedding hall was filled with dinner guests - Mt. 22:10.

# 12      Gather the people, sanctify the congregation.
          Assemble the elders;
          Gather the children and the nursing infants - Joel 2:16.

# 13      "But when the king came in to look over the dinner guests,
          he saw there a man not dressed in wedding clothes  - Mt. 22:11.

# 14-15   Let the bridegroom come out of his room,
          And the bride out of her bridal chamber - Joel 2:16.

# 16    Clothe yourself in your beautiful garments - Is. 52:1.

# 17    And clothe yourself with honor and majesty - Job. 40:10.

# 18    "But yield to the Lord and enter His sanctuary" - 2 Chr. 30:8.

# 19    Make vows to the Lord your God and fulfill them - Ps. 76:11.

# 20-22    "Go forth, O daughters of Zion,
And gaze on King Solomon with the crown
With which his mother has crowned him
On the day of his wedding,
And on the day of his gladness of heart" - SS 3:11.

# 23-25    For I used to go along with the throng and lead them in procession to the house of God,
With the voice of joy and thanksgiving - Ps. 42:4.

# 26    They will be led forth with gladness and rejoicing - Ps. 45:15.

# 27    "Lift up your eyes round about, and see" - Is. 60:4.

# 28    MW

# 29    The upright see it, and are glad - Ps. 107:42.

# 30    She will be led to the king in embroidered work - Ps. 45:14.

# 31    Can a virgin forget her ornaments,
Or a bride her attire? - Jer. 2:32.

# 32-33    I was glad when they said to me,
"Let us go to the house of the Lord" - Ps. 122:1.

# 34    "He who has the bride is the bridegroom" - Jn. 3:29.

# 35    MW

# 36    "Thou wilt make me full of gladness with Thy presence"
        - Ac. 2:28.

# 37    "And he who beholds Me beholds the One who sent Me"
        - Jn. 12:45.

# 38    In Thy presence is fullness of joy - Ps. 16:11.

# 39-41  I have set the Lord continually before me;
        Because He is at my right hand, I will not be shaken.
        Therefore my heart is glad, and my glory rejoices
        - Ps. 16:8-9.

# 42    Moreover my flesh also will abide in hope - Ac. 2:26.

# 43    Make vows to the Lord your God and fulfill them - Ps. 76:11.

# 44    "Also, if a woman makes a vow to the Lord, and binds
        herself by an obligation" - Num. 30:3.

# 45    "She is your companion and your wife by covenant"
        - Mal. 2:14.

# 46    For the married woman is bound by law to her husband
        while he is living - Rom. 7:2.

# 47    We love, because He first loved us - 1 Jn. 4:19.

# 48    "You shall love your neighbor as yourself" - Js. 2:8.

# 49-51   "For this commandment which I command you today is not too difficult for you, nor is it out of reach" - Deu. 30:11.

# 52-54   "But the word is very near you, in your mouth and in your heart, that you may observe it" - Deu. 30:14.

# 55-56   Then Moses said "Dedicate yourselves today to the Lord . . . in order that He may bestow a blessing upon you today" - Ex. 32:29.

# 57-58   Wives, be subject to your own husbands, as to the Lord - Eph. 5:22

# 59-60   "Then all women will give honor to their husbands, great and small" - Es. 1:20.

# 61-64   "Because my life was precious in your sight this day" - 1 Sam. 26:21.

# 65   "By your life and the life of your soul" - 2 Sam. 11:11.

# 66-67   "Please say that you are my sister so that it may go well with me because of you, and that I may live on account of you" - Gen. 12:13.

# 68-69   They will come that they may join themselves to the Lord in an everlasting covenant that will not be forgotten - Jer. 50:5.

# 70-72   "May the Lord be a true and faithful witness against us, if we do not act in accordance with the whole message with which the Lord your God will send you to us" - Jer. 42:5.

# 73   MW

# 74    MW, wedding vows based on the vows the author made in an Episcopal Church in 1951.

# 75    MW, ibid

#76-77    And the king stood by the pillar and made a covenant before the Lord - 2 K 23:3.

# 78    There will be silence before Thee - Ps. 65:1.

# 79    "If a man makes a vow to the Lord . . . Also if a woman makes a vow to the Lord" - Num. 30:2, 3.

# 80    MW

# 81    "This is My commandment, that you love one another, just as I have loved you" - Jo. 15:12.

# 82    And all the people entered into the covenant - 2 K 23:3.

# 83-84    "I have made a covenant with My chosen" - Ps. 89:3.

# 85-86    "That you may know and understand that the Father is in Me, and I in the Father." - Jn. 10:38.

# 87    One God and Father of all who is over all and through all and in all - Eph. 4:6

# 88    A cord of three strands is not quickly torn apart - Eccl. 4:12.

# 89-90    "Consequently they are no longer two, but one flesh. What therefore God has joined together, let no man separate" - Mk. 10:9.

# 91    For the Lord has done great things - Joel 2:21.

# 92-95  "Know therefore that the Lord your God, He is God, the faithful God, who keeps His covenant and His loving-kindness to a thousandth generation with those who love Him and keep His commandments" - Deu. 7:9.

# 96  MW

# 97  Greet one another with a holy kiss - 1 Cor. 16:20.

# 98  MW

# 99-100  "And I will make a covenant with them . . . to do them good" - Jer. 32:40.

# 101-102  "This is now bone of my bones,
And flesh of my flesh" - 2 Gen. 2:23.

# 103  MW

# 104  So we, who are many, are one body in Christ, and individually members one of another - Rom. 12:5.

# 105  "I will never break My covenant with you" - Judg. 2:1.

# 106-107  "As the Lord lives and as you yourself live, I will not leave you" - 2 K 2:2.

# 108-109  "Therefore deal kindly with your servant, for you have brought your servant into a covenant of the Lord with you" - 1 Sam. 20:8.

# 110  "As for the agreement of which you and I have spoken, behold, the Lord is between you and me forever" - 1 Sam. 20:23.

#111      I shall pay Thee my vows,
Which my lips uttered,
And my mouth spoke - Ps. 66:13-14.

#112-113    "For I will not leave you until I have done what I have
promised you" - Gen. 28:15.

#114-115    "You shall therefore impress these words of mine on
your heart and on your soul" - Deu. 11:18.

#116-122    "Only give heed to yourself and keep your soul diligently,
lest you forget the things which your eyes have seen, and
lest they depart from your heart all the days of your life;
but make them known to your sons and your grandsons"
- Deu. 4:9.

#123-125    For this reason, I bow my knees before the Father, from
whom every family in heaven and on earth derives its
name - Eph. 3:14-15.

#126-127    These are the statutes which the Lord commanded
Moses, as between a man and his wife, and as between a
father and his daughter, while she is in her youth in her
father's house - Num. 30:16.

#128-129    "No longer shall your name be called Abram" - Gen. 17:5.

#130-131    And you will be called by a new name,
Which the mouth of the Lord will designate - Is. 62:2

#132      "This is the sign of the covenant" - Gen. 9:17.

#133      That they will say, "This is his wife" - Gen. 12:12.

# 134    "My beloved is mine, and I am his" - SS 2:16.

# 135    "Since his life is bound up in the lad's life" - Gen. 44:30.

# 136    "But what I do have I give to you" - Ac. 3:6.

# 137-138    "Keep them in Thy name, the name which Thou hast given Me, that they may be one, even as We are" - Jn. 17:11.

# 139-140    "He took pleasure in me to make me king over all Israel" - 1 Chr. 28:4.

# 141-142    Then Pharaoh took off his signet ring from his hand and put it on Joseph's hand - Gen. 41:42.

# 143-144    "And behold, he pledged his allegiance" - Ezek. 17:18.

# 145    MW

# 146    Because he loved him as he loved his own life - 1 Sam. 20:17.

# 147-148    "My chosen one in whom My soul delights" - Is. 42:1.

# 149-152    "I am the Lord, I have called you in righteousness . . . And I will appoint you as a covenant to the people, As a light to the nations" - Is. 42:6.

# 153    "I am the Lord, that is My name" - Is. 42:8.

# 154-155    MW

# 156-157    "But we will certainly carry out every word that has proceeded from our mouths" - Jer. 44:17.

\# 158-159  "And I will keep You and give You for a covenant of the people, to restore the land" - Is. 49:8.

\# 160  MW

\# 161-162  "Be faithful until death, and I will give you the crown of life" - Rev. 2:10.

\# 163-164  "So you are My witnesses," declares the Lord, "And I am God" - Is. 43:12.

\# 165  And they said, "We are witnesses" - Josh. 24:22.

\# 166  "And we are witnesses of these things" - Ac. 5:32.

\# 167-170  Are joining with their kinsmen, their nobles, and are taking on themselves . . . an oath to walk in God's law . . . and to keep and to observe all the commandments of God our Lord - Neh. 10:29.

\# 171-172  Let a man regard us in this manner, as servants of Christ, and stewards of the mysteries of God - 1 Cor. 4:1.

\# 173-174  Guard, through the Holy Spirit who dwells in us, the treasure which has been entrusted to you - 2 Tim 1:14.

\# 175-178  Even though it is only a man's covenant, yet when it has been ratified, no one sets it aside or adds conditions to it - Gal. 3:15.

\# 179-180  For we shall all stand before the judgment seat of God - Rom. 14:10.

\# 181  So then each one of us shall give account of himself to God - Rom. 14:12.

# 182      MW

# 183      Applying all diligence, in your faith supply moral excellence - 2 Pet. 1:5.

# 184-185  Being diligent to preserve the unity of the Spirit in the
           bond of peace - Eph. 4:3.

# 186      But sanctify Christ as Lord in your hearts - 1 Pet. 3:15.

# 187-192  Now may the God of peace Himself sanctify you entirely;
           and may your spirit and soul and body be preserved complete,
           without blame at the coming of our Lord Jesus Christ - 1 Th. 5:23.

# 193      MW

# 194      And grant her honor as a fellow heir of the grace of life - 1 Pet. 3:7.

# 195      To which among the trees of Eden are you thus equal in
           glory and greatness? - Ezek. 31:18.

# 196      "The voice of joy and the voice of gladness" - Jer. 7:34.

# 197      MW

# 198-199  "The voice of the bridegroom and the voice of the bride" - Jer. 7:34.

# 200-203  "The voice of those who say,
           'Give thanks to the lord of hosts,
           For the Lord is good,
           For His lovingkindness is everlasting' " - Jer. 7:34.

END NOTES
PART 4: *Marriage*

# 1-4     "Look among the nations! Observe!
Be astonished! Wonder!
Because I am doing something in your days –
You would not believe if you were told" - Hab. 1:5.

# 5-7     You also, as living stones, are being built up as a spiritual
house for a holy priesthood, to offer up spiritual sacrifices
acceptable to God through Jesus Christ - 1 Pet. 2:5.

# 8     "He shall build a house for My name" - 2 Sam. 7:13.

# 9     Righteousness and justice are the foundation of Thy throne
- Ps. 89:14.

# 10-11     "But you shall call your walls salvation,
And your gates praise" - Is. 60:18.

# 12     "But the sound of singing I hear" - Ex. 32:18.

# 13     "And as you enter the house, give it your greeting"
- Mt. 10:12.

# 14     How lovely are Thy dwelling places! - Ps. 84:1.

# 15     "And now let Pharaoh look for a man discerning and wise"
- Gen. 41:33.

# 16     "Your dwelling place is enduring" - Num. 24:21.

# 17  I will walk within my house in the integrity of my heart
- Ps. 101:2.

# 18-20 And the work of righteousness will be peace,
And the service of righteousness, quietness and confidence
forever - Is. 32:17.

# 21  "For where two or three have gathered together in My
name, I am there in their midst" - Mt. 18:20.

# 22  These are the only fellow workers for the kingdom of God
- Col. 4:11.

# 23-27 "Bring the whole tithe into the storehouse so that there
may be food in My house, and test Me now in this," says
the Lord of hosts, "if I will not open for you the windows
of heaven, and pour out for you a blessing until it
overflows" - Mal. 3:10.

# 28  O Lord, I love the habitation of Thy house - Ps. 26:8.

# 29  "Surely the Lord is in this place, and I did not know it"
- Gen. 28:16.

# 30  MW

# 31-33 And the Lord God planted a garden toward the east, in
Eden; and there He placed the man whom He had formed.
And out of the ground the Lord God caused to grow every
tree that is pleasing to the sight and good for food
- Gen. 2:8-9.

# 34  MW

# 35      So we might walk in newness of life - Rom. 6:4b.

# 36      "And many evils and troubles shall come upon them"
             - Deu. 31:17.

# 37      "For it is inevitable that stumbling blocks come" - Mt. 18:7.

# 38-39      "The flowers have already appeared in the land;
             the time has arrived for pruning the vines" - SS 2:12.

# 40      They said therefore to Him, "What shall we do, that we may
             work the works of God?" - Jn. 6:28.

# 41      "For those who honor Me I will honor" - 1 Sam. 2:30.

# 42      God said further to Abraham, "Now as for you, you shall keep
             My covenant" - Gen. 17:9.

# 43-44      Why are you in despair, O my soul?
             And why have you become disturbed within me? - Ps. 42:5.

# 45      "For the ear tests words,
             As the palate tastes food" - Job 34:3.

# 46      "Let her alone, for her soul is troubled within her" - 2 K 4:27.

# 47      Giving no cause for offense in anything - 2 Cor. 6:3.

# 48      And see if there be any hurtful way in me - Ps. 139:24.

# 49      I pour out my complaint before Him - Ps. 142:2.

# 50      "Please let there be no strife between you and me"
             - Gen. 13:8.

# 51-52   So they piled them in heaps, and the land became foul
          - Ex. 8:14.

# 53-54   No temptation has overtaken you but such as is common
          to man - 1 Cor. 10:13.

# 55-57   Now I exhort you, brethren, by the name of our Lord
          Jesus Christ, that you all agree, and there be no divisions
          among you - 1 Cor. 1:10.

# 58      And the valley of Achor as a door of hope - Hos. 2:15.
          (note: the Hebrew word 'achor' means 'trouble' or 'troubled,'
          therefore one sees the valley of "Trouble" as a door of Hope.)

# 59-63   "If I have despised the claim of my male or female slaves,
          When they filed a complaint against me,
          What then could I do when God arises,
          And when He calls me to account,
          What shall I answer Him?" - Job 31:13-14.

# 64      "If therefore you are presenting your offering at the altar,
          and there remember that our brother has something against
          you" - Mt. 5:23.

# 65      Do not let the sun go down on your anger - Eph. 4:26.

# 66      "First be reconciled to your brother, and then come and
          present your offering" - Mt. 5:24.

# 67-69   [Love] bears all things, believes all things, hopes all things,
          endures all things. Love never fails - 1 Cor. 13:7-8.

#70-74    "For the mountains may be removed and the hills may shake,
But My loving-kindness will not be removed from you,
And My covenant of peace will not be shaken,"
Says the Lord who has compassion on you - Is. 54:10.

#75-76    "Arise, my darling, my beautiful one,
And come along" - SS 2:10.

#77    "Her soul is troubled within her" - 2 K 4:27.

#78    "And if your brother sins, go and reprove him in private"
- Mt. 18:15.

#79    "Because the Lord has been a witness between you and the
wife of your youth" - Mal. 2:14.

#80-81    For God is greater than our heart, and knows all things
- 1 Jo. 3:20.

#82    "Make friends quickly with your opponent" - Mt. 5:25.

#83-85    Therefore, confess your sins to one another, and pray for
one another, so that you may be healed - Js. 5:16.

#86    "I have heard the complaints of the sons of Israel, which
they are making against Me" - Num. 14:27.

#87    And David said to God, "I have sinned greatly, in that I
have done this thing" - 1 Chr. 21:8.

#88    "Please forgive, I beg you, the transgression of your brothers
and their sin, for they did you wrong" - Gen. 50:17.

# 89    "But now, please take away the iniquity of Thy servant"
- 1 Chr. 21:8.

# 90    "For has anyone said to God,
'I have borne chastisement;
I will not offend anymore'?" - Job 34:31.

# 91-92    God was in Christ reconciling the world to Himself, not
counting their trespasses against them, and He has committed
to us the word of reconciliation - 2 Cor. 5:19.

# 93    Then the chief cupbearer spoke to Pharaoh, saying, "I would
make mention today of my own offenses" - Gen. 41:9.

# 94-95    Bearing with one another, and forgiving each other
- Col. 3:13.

# 96-97    MW

# 98    And Moab will be trodden down in his place
As straw is trodden down in the water of a manure pile
- Is. 25:10.

# 99    While I am decaying like a rotten thing - Job 13:28.

# 100    "He also took some of the seed of the land and planted it in
fertile soil" -Ezek. 17:5

# 101    "Let the earth sprout vegetation" - Gen. 1:11.

# 102-103    And they seized upon that statement, discussing with one
another what rising from the dead might mean - Mk. 9:10.

# 104-105    MW

# 106-107    Above all, keep fervent in your love for one another, because love covers a multitude of sins - 1 Pet. 4:8.

# 108    Now all these things are from God, who reconciled us to Himself through Christ and gave us the ministry of reconciliation - 2 Cor. 5:18.

# 109-110    And if he has committed sins, they will be forgiven him - Js. 5:15.

# 111-112    And beyond all these things put on love, which is the perfect bond of unity - Col. 3:14.

# 113-116    "For as the rain and the snow come down from heaven, And do not return there without watering the earth, And making it bear and sprout" - Is. 55:10.

# 117    MW

# 118    His shoots will sprout - Hos. 14:6.

# 119    MW

# 120-124    "Drip down, O heavens, from above, And let the clouds pour down righteousness; Let the earth open up and salvation bear fruit, And righteousness spring up with it" - Is.45:8

# 125-126    How much more will the blood of Christ . . . cleanse your conscience from dead works to serve the living God? - Heb. 9:14.

# 127-128    And after you have suffered for a little while, the God of all grace . . . will Himself perfect, confirm, strengthen and establish you - 1 Pet. 5:10.

# 129-131   But thanks be to God, who always leads us in His triumph in Christ, and manifests through us the sweet aroma of the knowledge of Him in every place
- 2 Cor. 2:14.

# 132   For we are a fragrance of Christ to God among those who are being saved and among those who are perishing
- 2 Cor. 2:15.

# 133-134   Consequently we urged Titus that as he had previously made a beginning, so he would also complete in you this gracious work as well - 2 Cor. 8:6.

# 135   I am not speaking this as a command, but as proving through the earnestness of others the sincerity of your love also - 2 Cor. 8:8.

# 136-137   Who were the first to begin a year ago not only to do this, but also to desire to do it - 2 Cor. 8:10.

# 138-141   But now finish doing it also; that just as there was the readiness to desire it, so there may be also the completion of it by your ability - 2 Cor. 8:11.

# 142   Or the wife you cherish . . . who is as your own soul
- Deu. 13:6.

# 143   Do you not know that your bodies are members of Christ?
- 1 Cor. 6:15.

# 144   We who had sweet fellowship together - Ps. 55:14.

# 145-146   I weep . . . Because far from me is a comforter, One who restores my soul - Lam. 1:16.

# 147    The help of my countenance, and my God - Ps. 42:11.

#148    But it is you, a man my equal, My companion and my familiar friend - Ps. 53:13.

# 149-151    So that you may walk in a manner worthy of the God who calls you into His own kingdom and glory - 1 Th. 2:12.

# 152    Since you have in obedience to the truth purified your souls for a sincere love of the brethren - 1 Pet. 1:22.

# 153    And sustain me with a willing spirit - Ps. 51:12.

# 154    MW

# 155-156    Wives, be subject to your husbands, as is fitting in the Lord - Col. 3:18.

# 157-160    Whatever you do, do your work heartily, as for the Lord rather than for men; knowing that from the Lord you will receive the reward of the inheritance - Col. 3:23-24.

# 161-162    So I called the priests and took an oath from them that they would do according to this promise - Neh. 5:12.

# 163-164    In all our distress and affliction we were comforted about you through your faith - 1 Th. 3:7.

# 165-166    Be on the alert, stand firm in the faith, act like men, be strong - 1 Cor. 16:13.

# 167    An excellent wife is the crown of her husband - Pr. 12:4.

\# 168-169   Then our mouth was filled with laughter,
          And our tongue with joyful shouting;
          Then they said among the nations,
          "The Lord has done great things for them" - Ps. 126:2.

\# 170-171   The Lord has done great things for us;
          We are glad - Ps. 126:3.

\# 172-175   "But as for you, go your way to the end; then you will enter into rest and rise again for your allotted portion at the end of the age" - Dan. 12:13.

# END NOTES
## PART 5: *Reward*

**# 1-5**    Yet those who wait for the Lord
Will gain new strength;
They will mount up with wings like eagles,
They will run and not get tired.
They will walk and not become weary - Is. 40:31.

**# 6-7**    "Who is this coming up from the wilderness,
Leaning on her beloved?" - SS 8:5.

**# 8-9**    "Come back, come back, that we may gaze at you!"
- SS 6:13.

**# 10**    "Those who see you will gaze at you;
They will ponder over you" - Is. 14:16.

**# 11**    MW

**# 12-13**    Older men are to be temperate, dignified, sensible, sound
in faith, in love, in perseverance - Tit. 2:2.

**# 14-15**    "Why should you gaze at the Shulammite,
As at the dance of the two companies?" - SS 6:13.

**# 16-19**    Who crowns you with loving-kindness and compassion;
Who satisfies your years with good things,
So that your youth is renewed like the eagle - Ps. 103:4-5.

# 20    "I am an old man, and my wife is advanced in years"
        - Lu. 1:18

        "Rich toward God" - Lu. 12:21.

# 21-22  Not boasting beyond our measure, . . . but with the hope
        that as your faith grows, we shall be, within our sphere, enlarged
        even more by you - 2 Cor. 10:15.

# 23    "I am still as strong today as I was in the day Moses sent
        me" - Josh. 14:11.

# 24    MW

# 25-28  For he will not often consider the years of his life, because
        God keeps him occupied with the gladness of his heart
        - Eccl. 5:20.

# 29-31  Behold, the Lord God will come with might,
        With His arm ruling for Him.
        Behold, His reward is with Him,
        And His recompense before Him - Is. 40:10.

# 32    For the day of the Lord is coming - Joel 2:1.

# 33-34  So then each one of us shall give account of himself to
        God - Rom.14:12.

# 35    "What shall I say to them?" - Ex. 3:13.

# 36    MW

#37-41     "Now therefore, our God, the great, the mighty, and the awesome God, who dost keep covenant and loving-kindness, Do not let all the hardship seem insignificant before Thee, which has come upon us" - Neh. 9:32.

# 42     MW

# 43-45     "However, Thou are just in all that has come upon us; For Thou hast dealt faithfully, but we have acted wickedly" - Neh. 9:33.

# 46     "Had it not been the Lord who was on our side" - Ps. 124:1.

# 47     No temptation has overtaken you but such as is common to man - 1 Cor. 10:13.

# 48     The one who commits adultery with a woman is lacking sense; He who would destroy himself does it - Pr. 6:32.

# 49     You have not given me over into the hand of the enemy - Ps. 31:8.

# 50     But each one is tempted when he is carried away and enticed by his own lust - Js. 1:14

# 51-52     The Lord knows how to rescue the godly from temptation - 2 Pet. 2:9.

# 53     "For I have kept the ways of the Lord" - 2 Sam. 22:22.

# 54-58    By faith Moses, when he had grown up, refused to be called the son of Pharaoh's daughter; choosing rather to endure ill-treatment with the people of God, than to enjoy the passing pleasures of sin; considering the reproach of Christ greater riches than the treasures of Egypt; for he was looking to the reward. - Heb. 11:24-6.

# 59-60    For he endured as seeing Him who is unseen - Heb. 11:27.

# 61    If the Lord had not been my help - Ps. 94:17.

# 62    For forty days, being tempted by the devil - Lu. 4:2.

# 63-64    My soul would soon have dwelt in the abode of silence - Ps. 94:17.

# 65-66    Resist the devil and he will flee from you - Js. 4:7.

# 67-70    Our soul has escaped as a bird out of the snare of the trapper; The snare is broken and we have escaped - Ps. 124:7.

# 71    MW

# 72    Are you bound to a wife? Do not seek to be released - 1 Cor. 7:27.

# 73    Thou art good and doest good - Ps. 119:68.

# 74    "In the wilderness He fed you manna which your fathers did not know, that He might humble you and that He might test you, to do good for you in the end" - Deu. 8:16.

# 75    The fear of the Lord is the beginning of wisdom - Ps. 111:10.

# 76-77    How blessed is everyone who fears the Lord, Who walks in His ways - Ps. 128:1.

\# 78-79 The elder to the chosen lady and her children, whom we love in truth - 2 Jn. 1.

\# 80 Older women likewise are to be reverent in their behavior ... teaching what is good - Tit. 2:3.

\# 81-82 So that you may walk in a manner worthy of the Lord to please Him in all respects - Col. 1:10.

\# 83-84 In Him we have redemption through His blood, the forgiveness of our trespasses, according to the riches of His grace - Eph. 1:7.

\# 85-87 Walk in love, just as Christ also loved you, and gave Himself up for us - Eph. 5:2.

\# 88-90 Bless our God, O peoples,
And sound His praise abroad,
Who keeps us in life - Ps. 66:8-9.

\# 91-92 Bless the Lord, O my soul;
And all that is within me, bless His holy name - Ps. 103:1.

\# 93-94 Bless the Lord, O my soul,
And forget none of His benefits - Ps. 103:2.

\# 95-99 "For I say to you, that many prophets and kings wished to see the things which you see, and did not see them, and to hear the things which you hear, and did not hear them" - Lu. 10:24.

\# 100 Furthermore, the man Moses himself was greatly esteemed in the land of Egypt - Ex. 11:3.

# 101     And respectful greetings in the market places - Mt. 23:7.

# 102-103   "So you too, when you do all the things which are commanded you, say, 'We are unworthy slaves; we have done only that which we ought to have done' " - Lu. 17:10.

# 104     Then the Lord said to Moses, "Behold the time for you to die is near" - Deu. 31:14.

# 105     MW

# 106-108   Be transformed by the renewing of your mind that you may prove what the will of God is, that which is good and acceptable and perfect - Rom. 12:2.

#109     "Prepare to meet your God, O Israel" - Am. 4:12.

#110     MW

# 111     For I know your readiness - 2 Cor. 9:2.

# 112-113   MW

# 114-116   But I have sent the brethren, that our boasting about you may not be made empty in this case, that, as I was saying, you may be prepared - 2 Cor. 9:3.

# 117     So I thought it necessary to urge the brethren that they would go on ahead to you and arrange beforehand your previously promised bountiful gift - 2 Cor. 9:5.

# 118-124 By faith Noah, being warned by God about thing not yet seen, in reverence prepared an ark for the salvation of his household, by which he condemned the world, and became an heir of the righteousness which is according to faith - Heb. 11:7.

# 125-128 Therefore, let us fear lest, while a promise remains of entering His rest, any one of you should seem to have come short of it - Heb. 4:1.

# 129-131 And now, little children, abide in Him, so that when He appears, we may have confidence and not shrink away from Him in shame at His coming - 1 Jn. 2:28.

# 132-134 "Gather My godly ones to Me,
Those who have made a covenant with Me by sacrifice"
- Ps. 50:5

# 135 Our soul waits for the Lord - Ps. 33:20.

# 136-137 Inasmuch as it is appointed for men to die once and after comes judgment - Heb. 9:27.

# 138-139 Because He has fixed a day in which He will judge the world in righteousness through a Man whom He has appointed - Ac. 17:31.

# 140-141 MW

# 142 Has His promise come to an end forever? - Ps. 77:8.

# 143 MW

# 144    Where a covenant is, there must of necessity be the
death of the one who made it; for a covenant is valid only
when men are dead, for it is never in force while the one
who made it lives - Heb. 9:16-17.

# 145    "Truly, truly, I say to you, when you were younger, you used
to gird yourself, and walk wherever you wished; but when
you grow old, you will stretch out your hands, and someone
else will gird you" - Jn. 21:18.

# 146    MW

# 147    And they laid his body in his own grave - 1 K 13:30.

# 148    For He has clothed me with garments of salvation - Is. 61:10.

# 149-151    Now there was a day when the sons of God came to
present themselves before the Lord - Job 1:6.

# 152-154    And without faith it is impossible to please Him, for he
who comes to God must believe that He is, and that He
is a rewarder of those who seek Him - Heb. 11:6.

# 155-156    "In My Father's house are many dwelling places; . . . I go
to prepare a place for you" - Jn.14:2.

# 157    Behold, the Judge is standing right at the door - Js. 5:9.

# 158-159    "Once the head of the house gets up and shuts the door,
and you begin to stand outside and knock on the door,
saying, 'Lord, open up to us!' then He will answer . . ."
– Lu. 13:25.

\# 160-162    Open to me the gates of righteousness;
I shall enter through them,
I shall give thanks to the Lord - Ps. 118:19.

\# 163       "A voice! My beloved was knocking" - SS 5:2.

\# 164-165    Hearts are melting and knees knocking! - Nah. 2:10.

\# 166-167    Take care, brethren, lest there should be in anyone of you
an evil, unbelieving heart, in falling away from the living
God - Heb. 3:12.

\# 168-169    Say to those with anxious heart,
"Take courage and fear not" - Is. 35:4.

\# 170-172    "In every nation the man who fears Him and does what
is right, is welcome to Him" - Ac. 10:35.

\# 173-174    "And be like men who are waiting for their master when
he returns from the wedding feast so that they may
immediately open the door to him when he comes and
knocks" - Lu. 12:36.

\# 175       "My Lord and my God!" - Jn. 20:28.

\# 176-178    And it will be said in that day,
"Behold, this is our God for whom we have waited that
He might save us.
This is the Lord for whom we have waited;
Let us rejoice and be glad in His salvation" - Is. 25:9.

# 179-181   "Come now, and let us reason together,"
Says the Lord,
"Though your sins are as scarlet,
They will be as white as snow" - Is. 1:18.

# 182-184   "Behold I am coming quickly, and My reward is with Me,
to render to every man according to what he has done"
- Rev. 22:12.

# 185-186   But they shall give account to Him who is ready to judge
the living and the dead - 1 Pet. 4:5.

# 187-188   "And I say to you, that every careless word that men shall
speak, they shall render account for it in the day of
judgment" - Mt. 12:36.

# 189-190   "Present your case," the Lord says.
"Bring forward your strong arguments" - Is. 41:21.

# 191   "State your cause, that you may be proved right" - Is. 43:26.

# 192   "He said to him, 'By your own words I will judge you' "
- Lu. 19:22.

# 193-194   For all have sinned and fall short of the glory of God
- Rom. 3:23.

# 195-198   "Repent therefore and return, that your sins may be wiped
away, in order that times of refreshing may come from
the presence of the Lord" - Ac. 3:19.

# 199-200   The Lord of hosts has sworn saying, "Surely, just as I
have intended, so it has happened" - Is. 14:24.

# 201-203    But this is the covenant which I will make with the house of Israel after those days," declares the Lord, "I will put My law within them, and on their heart I will write it; and I will be their God, and they shall be My people" - Jer. 31:33.

# 204    For Thou hast tried us, O God - Ps. 66:10.

# 205-206    We went through fire and through water: Yet Thou didst bring us out into a place of abundance - Ps. 66:12.

# 207-208    And we have come to know and have believed the love which God has for us - 1 Jn.4:16.

# 209-212    "Now then, if you will indeed obey My voice and keep My covenant, then you shall be My own possession among all the peoples" - Ex. 19:5.

# 213-214    "Not everyone who says to Me, 'Lord, Lord,' will enter the kingdom of heaven; but he who does the will of My Father who is in heaven" - Mt. 7:21.

# 215    His master said to him, "Well done, good and faithful servant" - Mt. 25:21.

# 216    MW

# 217    "Well done, good and faithful servant! . . . Enter into the joy of your master" - Mt. 25:21.

# 218    "Truly I say to you, today you shall be with Me in Paradise" - Lu. 23:43.

# 219-220    The men reached out their hands and brought Lot into
the house with them, and shut the door - Gen. 19:10.

# 221-224    Shout for joy, O daughter of Zion!
Shout in triumph, O Israel!
Rejoice and exult with all your heart,
O daughter of Jerusalem!
The Lord has taken away His judgments against you
- Zeph. 3:14-15.

# 225-226    "He will exult over you with joy,
He will rejoice over you with shouts of joy
- Zeph. 3:17.

# 227-230    I will rejoice greatly in the Lord,
My soul will exult in my God;
For He has clothed me with garments of salvation,
He has wrapped me with a robe of righteousness
- Is. 61:10.

# 231    "Well done, good and faithful servant! . . . Enter into the joy
of your master" - Mt. 25:21.

# 232    MW

# 233    A good man leaves an inheritance to his children's children
- Pr. 13:22.

# 234    That you may tell it to the next generation - Ps. 48:13.

# 235-237    That the generation to come might know, even the
children yet to be born,
That they may arise and tell them to their children
- Ps. 78:6.

# 238     MW

# 239-240  "I glorified Thee on the earth, having accomplished the work which Thou hast given Me to do" - Jn. 17:4.

# 241     He has also set eternity in their heart - Eccl. 3:11.

# 242     Having gained approval through their faith - Heb.11:39.

# 243-244  "For David, after he had served the purpose of God in his own generation" - Ac. 13:36.

# 245     Let marriage be held in honor among all - Heb. 13:4.

# 246     Thou wilt give truth to Jacob
And unchanging love to Abraham,
Which Thou didst swear to our forefathers
From the days of old - Mic. 7:20.

# 247     MW

# 248-249  "This is my beloved Son, with whom I am well pleased"
– Mt. 17:5.

# 250     And all the people shall say, "Amen" - Deu. 27:15-26.

.

# ABBREVIATIONS

| | | | |
|---|---|---|---|
| Genesis | Gen. | Matthew | Mt. |
| Exodus | Ex. | Mark | Mk. |
| Leviticu | Lev. | Luke | Lu. |
| Numbers | Num. | John | Jn. |
| Deuteronomy | Deu. | Acts | Ac. |
| Joshua | Josh. | Romans | Rom. |
| Judges | Judg. | First Corinthians | 1 Cor. |
| Ruth | Ru. | Second Corinthians | 2. Cor. |
| Samuel | Sam. | Galatians | Gal. |
| Kings | K | Ephesians | Eph. |
| Chronicles | Chr. | Philippians | Ph'p |
| Ezra | Ezr. | Colossians | Col. |
| Nehemiah | Neh. | First Thessalonians | 1 Th. |
| Esther | Es. | Second Thessalonians | 2 Th. |
| Job | Job | First Timothy | 1 Tim. |
| Psalms | Ps. | Second Timothy | 2 Tim. |
| Proverbs | Pr. | Titus | Tit. |
| Ecclesiastes | Eccl. | Philemon | Phil. |
| Song of Solomon | SS | Hebrews | Heb. |
| Isaiah | Is. | James | Js. |
| Jeremiah | Jer. | First Peter | 1 Pet. |
| Lamentations | Lam. | Second Peter | 2 Pet. |
| Ezekiel | Ezek. | First John | 1 Jn. |
| Daniel | Dan. | Second John | 2 Jn. |
| Hosea | Hos. | Third John | 3 Jn. |
| Joel | Joel | Jude | Jude |
| Amos | Am. | Revelation | Rev. |
| Obadiah | Ob. | | |
| Jonah | Jon. | | |
| Micah | Mic. | | |
| Nahum | Nah. | | |
| Habakkuk | Hab. | | |
| Zephaniah | Zeph. | | |
| Haggai | Hag. | | |
| Zechariah | Zech. | | |
| Malachi | Mal. | | |

# NOTES

# NOTES

NOTES

NOTES

Printed in Great Britain
by Amazon

26436351R00071